eBook ISBN 978-1-958503-12-6

Paperback ISBN 978-1-958503-10-2

Hardback ISBN 978-1-958503-11-9

GenZ Publishing LLC

Morganville, NJ

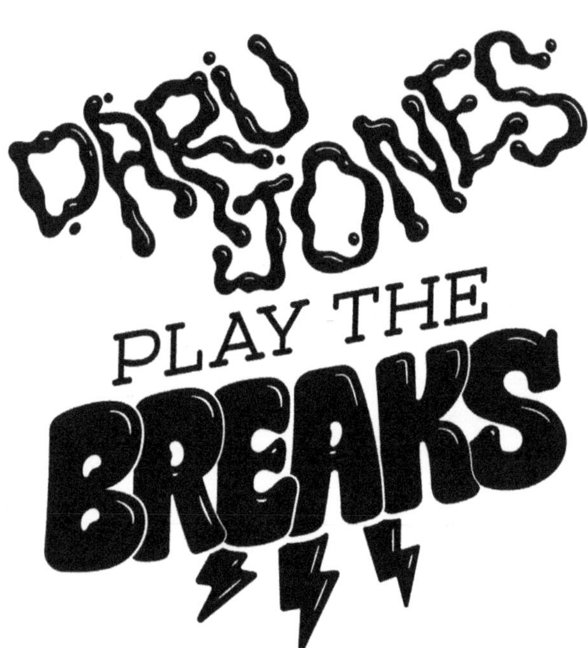

LIVE FROM LAYMAN

DELUXE EDITION

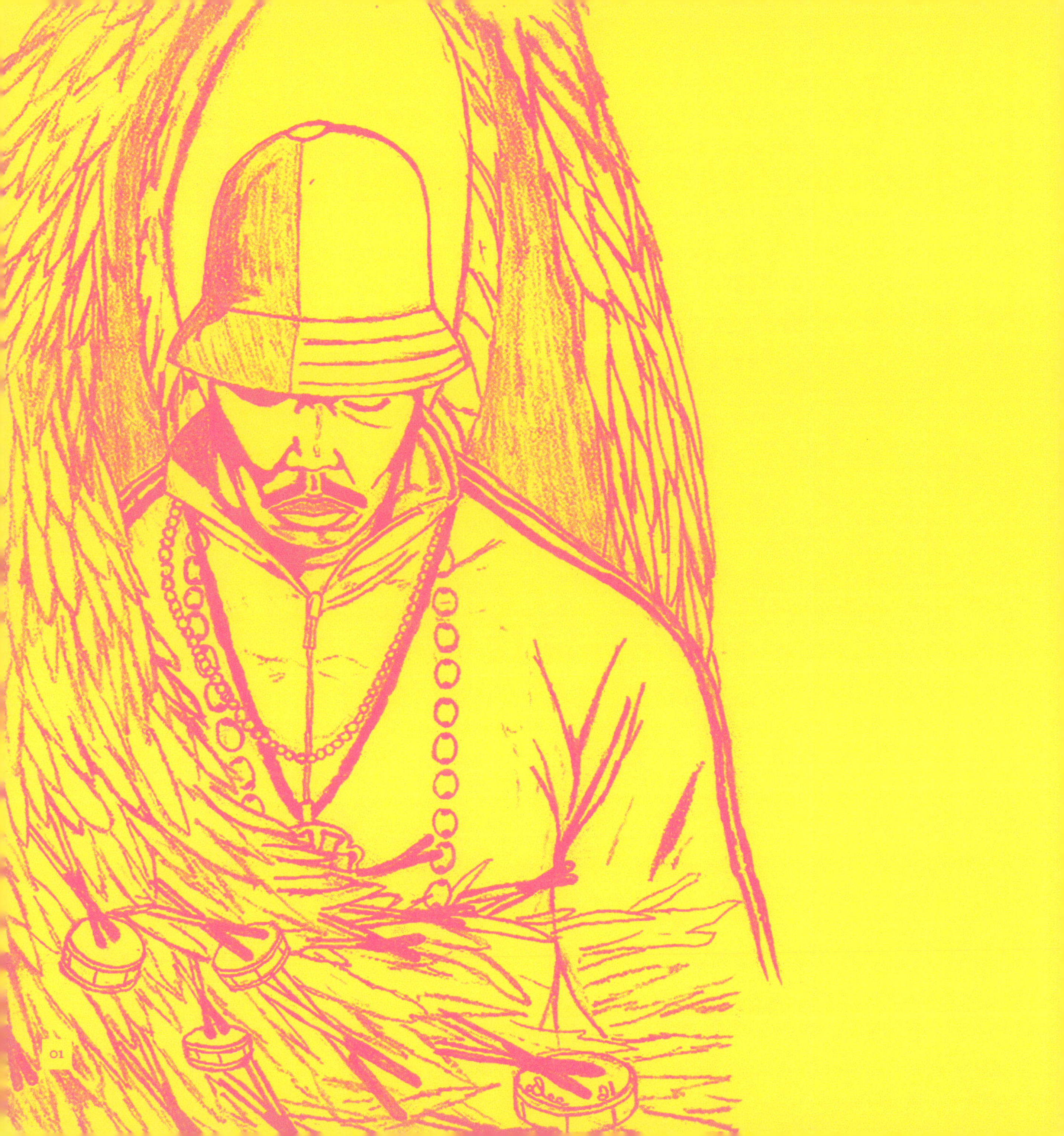

BREAKBEAT LOU "INTRO"

"*PLAY THE BREAKS*" by Daru Jones. Where do I start? Daru Jones has to have the heaviest foot on a kick drum that I've been able to witness live – in my life! His snares are so snappy and slappy that it's like you're getting slapped in the face fourteen times every time he hits it. This particular album shows the history of him rocking breaks for incredible artists. And me, being known for what I do, (meaning the breaks) there's nothing more satisfying to hear than this incredible, gifted musician display and tell you the story behind how he was inspired to create these pieces of what I call "mastepieces" as far as live drumming when it comes to Hip-Hop. So, as I always say when something means a lot to me or hits me hard – "*Daru Jones PLAY THE BREAKS Live*" is most definitely UBB APPROVED. Peace.

– BreakBeat Lou
Co-creator of the ***Ultimate Breaks & Beats Compilation***

Daru and Breakbeat Lou met during Funky Good Time at 5 Spot in Nashville, where Daru performed his signature idea of drumming with a DJ.

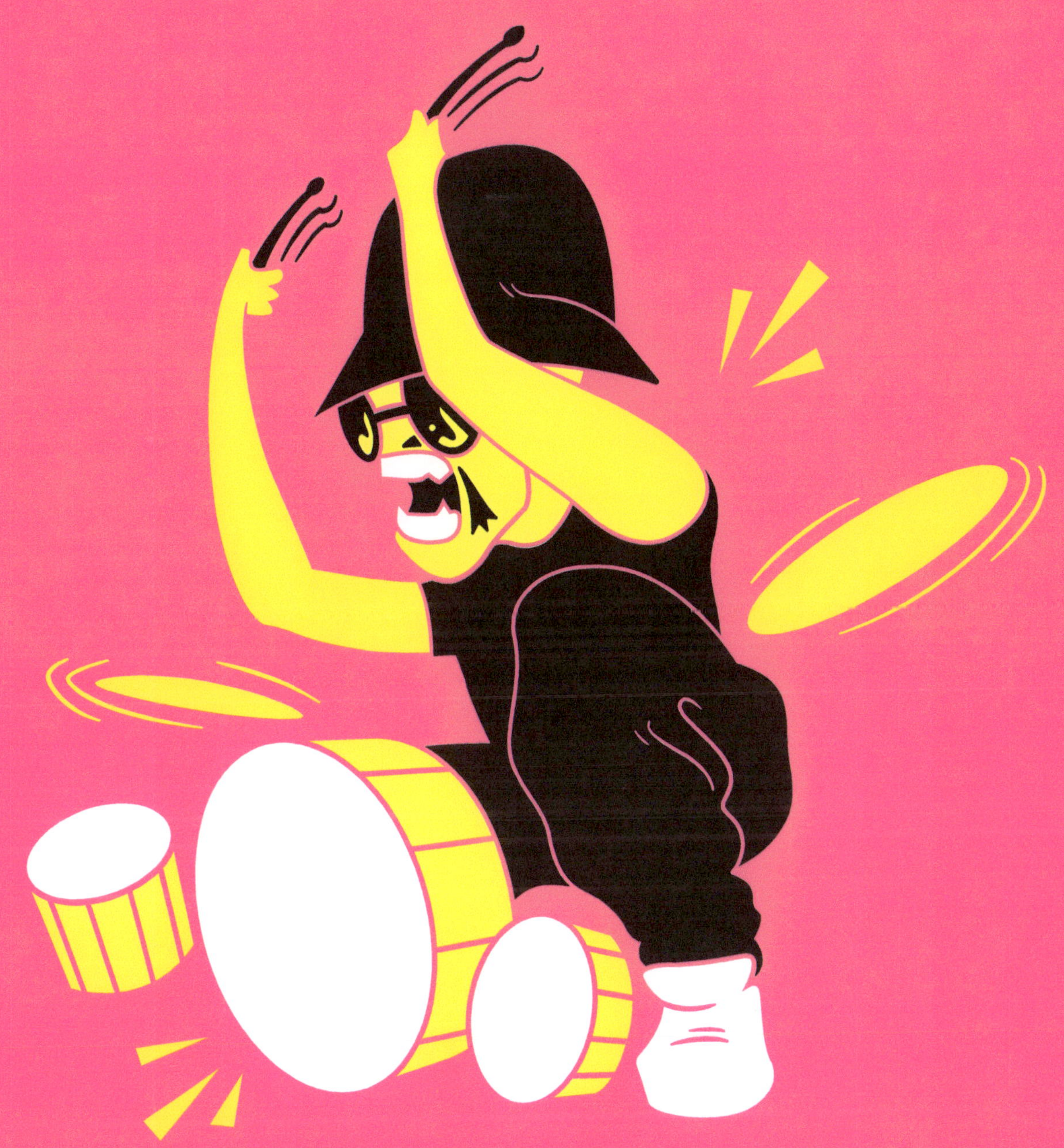

MILK
"2 WOULD TRY"

The name of this track is called "2 WOULD TRY". It features Dwele and it's from the album called "Fever" by Black Milk. We recorded it in Detroit, MI. The album came out 2018. Black had this pattern he had produced on his machine and I was jamming along with it. We found a pattern I was playing that he liked, and we chopped it up. He uses it. It comes in on the chorus also sporadically through the verses.

MILK
"KEEP GOING"

The name of this track is called "KEEP GOING" and it's from "Album of the Year" by Black Milk. We recorded this track in Detroit, MI in 2009. I remember this beat. It was on the Black Milk special beats CDs called "The Practice". I think that was the name of it. He had the pattern going and I thought of something to play on top. We both agreed on it. This track also features Al, and this was the first single from the album that came out in 2010.

Daru recorded this song during the Christmas break holiday when he went back home to Michigan to visit his family.

MILK
"TRUE LIES"

The name of the track is called "TRUE LIES" and it's from "Fever" by Black Milk. It was released 2018. I remember this track because we were in the studio in Detroit – Coltay Studio actually – and Black had brought in a couple session players (Sasha on guitar and Fink on Keys.) I told Black I was really listening to some Police with Stewart Copeland and Sting. This beat or rather the vibe of the music was inspired by those Police records. Definitely one of my favorite tracks from the album. Shout out to Stewart Copeland (one of my favorite drummers.) I played with his vibe, but with my swag.

MILK
"ROUND OF APPLAUSE"

The name of the track is "ROUND OF APPLAUSE" from "Album of the Year" by Black Milk (2010.) It's one of my favorite tracks. Black allowed me to shine a lot on this track. He was going for a Fela Kuti vibe with the horns. Fun track. He had a pattern he was playing that was similar to the groove and I just added my own extra vibes to it. Definitely one of my favorite tracks on the album.

Daru's drumming influences include: Dana Davis, Steve Gadd, Vinnie Colaiuta, Stewart Copeland, Steve Smith, Peter Eskine, Bernard Purdie, Virgil Donati,Dave Weckl, Tony Williams, Elvin Jones, Gene Krupa, Omar Hakim, Bill Maxwell, Questlove

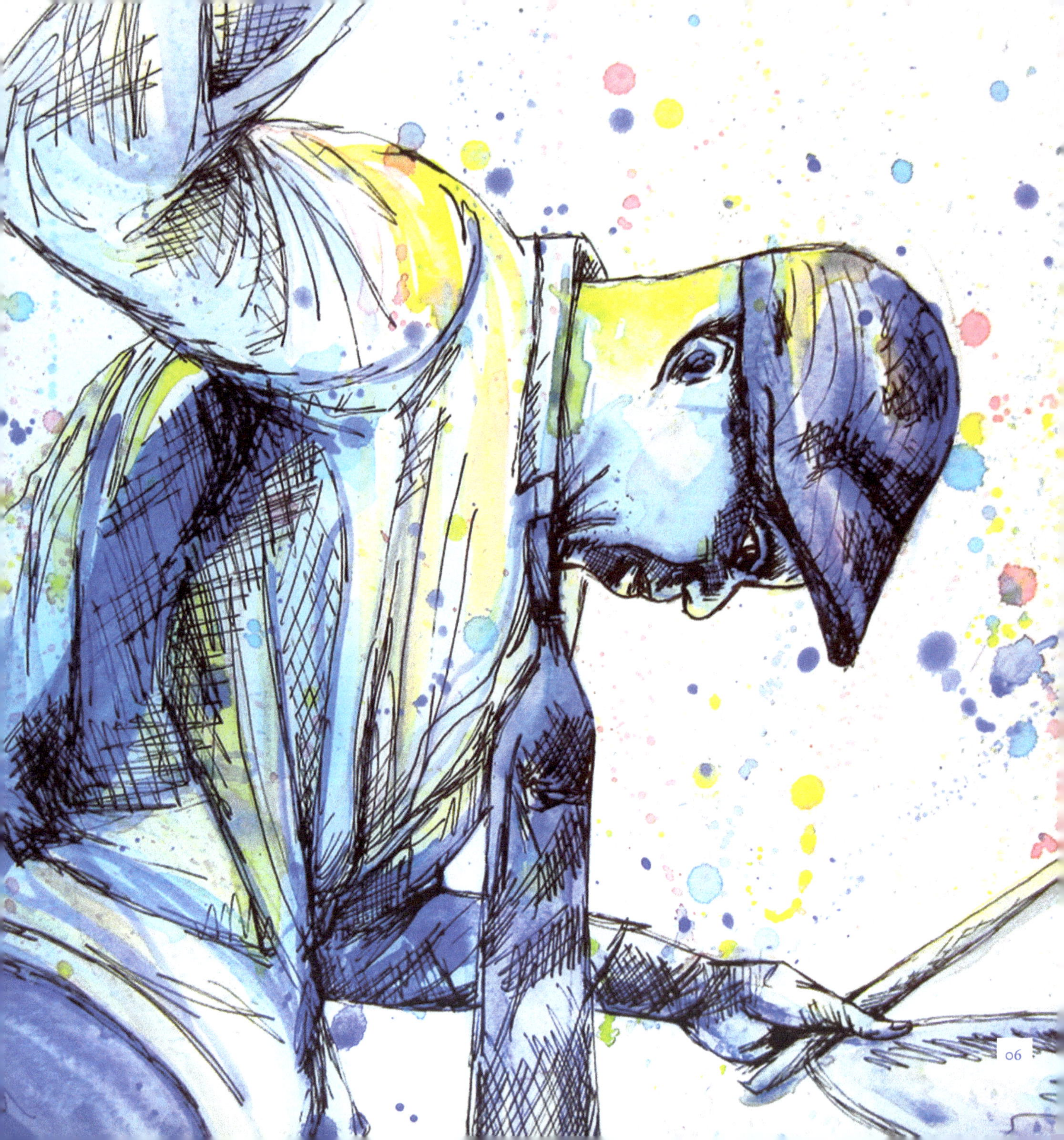

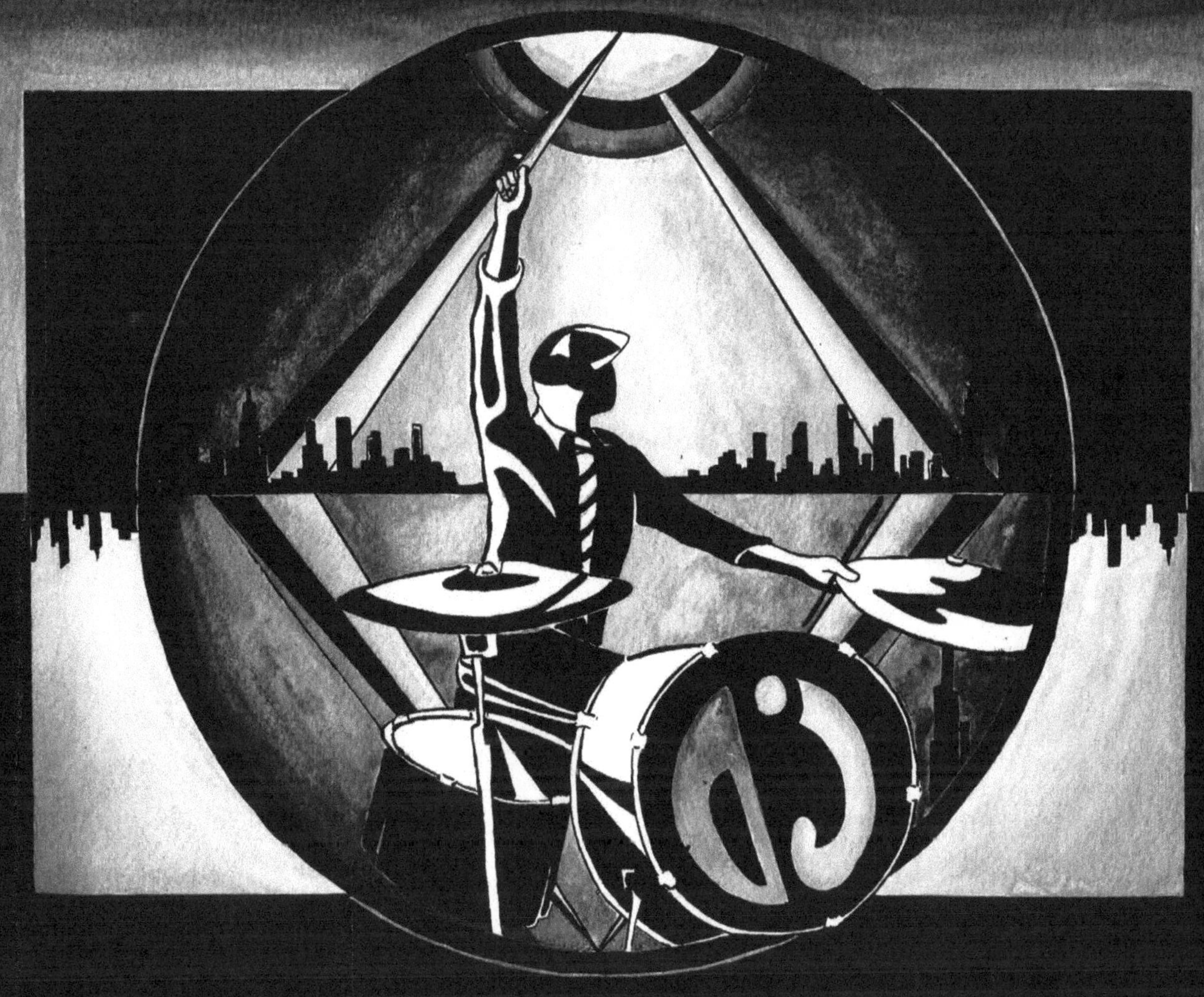

Daru started drumming at age 4. He knew in his teenage years that he wanted to be a genre-bending drummer.

MILK "CLOSED CHAPTER"

The track is called "CLOSED CHAPTER" and features Denaun Porter (Mr. Porter) from Detroit, MI. This is from "Album of the Year" by Black Milk. It was recorded at Studio 1 – Black Milk's studio – and we had fun with this one. I had just got in the studio and I heard him playing his samples with the beat that he produced, and I instantly just started playing a funky pattern around it. I think I did like... a hot 16 bars to 32 bars. If you hear it we just looped it every 32 bars. It's one of my favorite tracks too, and it's the last track on the album.

MILK "BRAIN"

The name of this song is called "BRAIN", and it came out 2010. This was the collaboration Jack White did with Black Milk. They did two tracks, and this is a track that I played on. This was an AMAZING session. I'll never forget it. Also, my introduction would make an impression on Jack for him to hire me in the future. Jack had his session players and then Black brought us down (myself, Malik, and AB because we were in his touring band) and we did a jam session for like 15 minutes. We heard the playback and the engineer Vance Powell cut the tape and slimmed it down to about 4 minutes, and Black Milk just rapped on top. That's all she wrote.

WHITE
"LAZARETTO"

The name of this track is called "LAZARETTO" and it's from Jack White's second solo album of the same name. This was a fun session. I remember I think we did this in 2013. We took a break between the tours (the Blunderbuss tours) and Jack had the ladies (the all-female band The Peacocks) in the studio for a couple days and then had the guys (the all-male band The Buzzards) and this is one of the tracks that we laid down. It was inspired by MC Lyte's "Cha Cha Cha". We were listening to that and Jack said let's make something like THIS. And this is what we came up with based around the drums.

WHITE
"INACCESSIBLE MYSTERY"

This is the B-Side for "FREEDOM AT 21" and the name of the track is called "INACCESSIBLE MYSTERY". It's one of the first tracks I recorded with Jack White in 2011, and this was a session we were supposed to do with RZA, but RZA cancelled. Jack said he had a couple solo songs that he was working on and this is what we came up with.

The Lazaretto performance on SNL was a last-minute opportunity. The audience gave it a standing ovation, and host Bill Burr joked about the position of Daru's drums before calling the performance 'face-melting'.

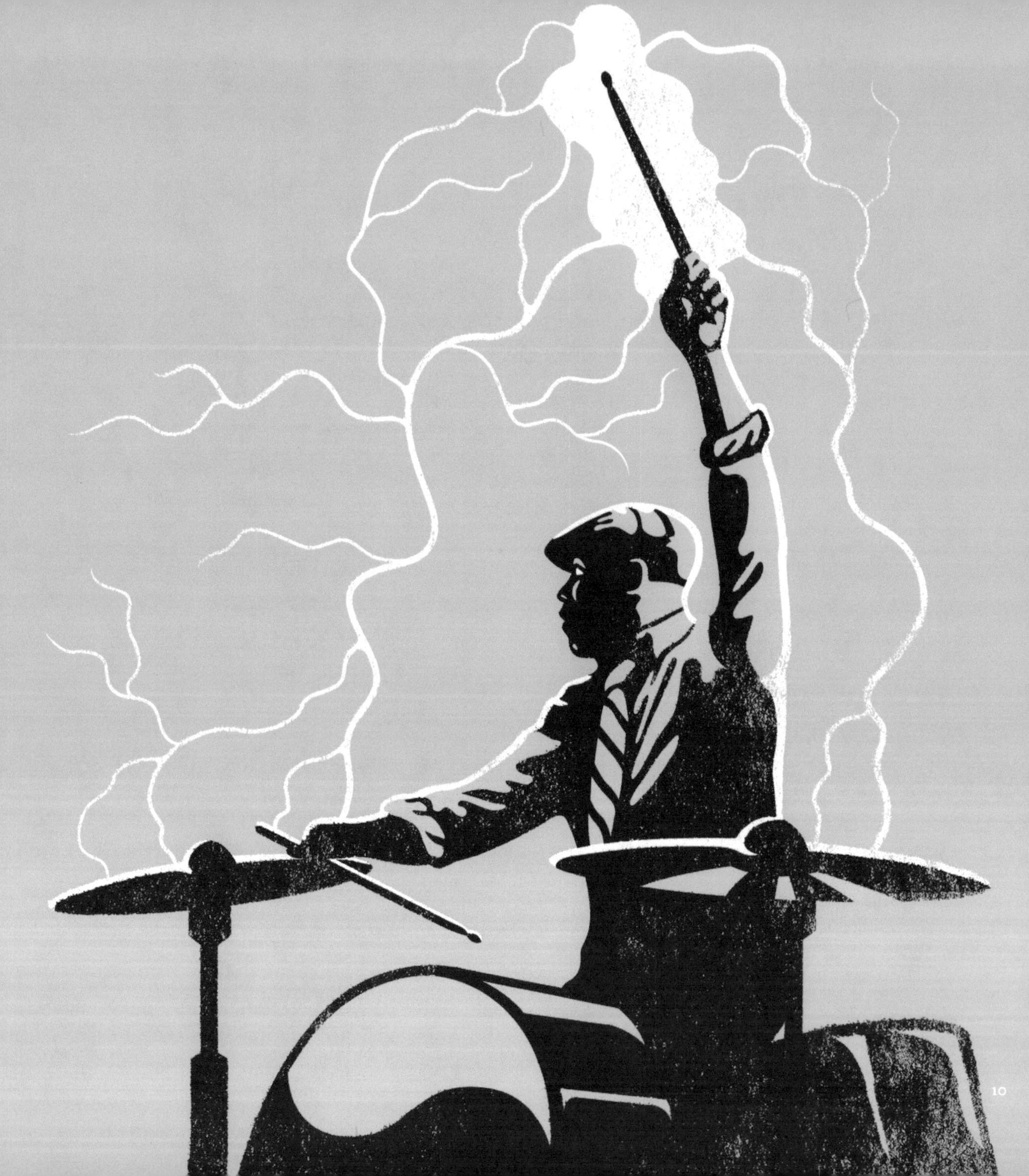

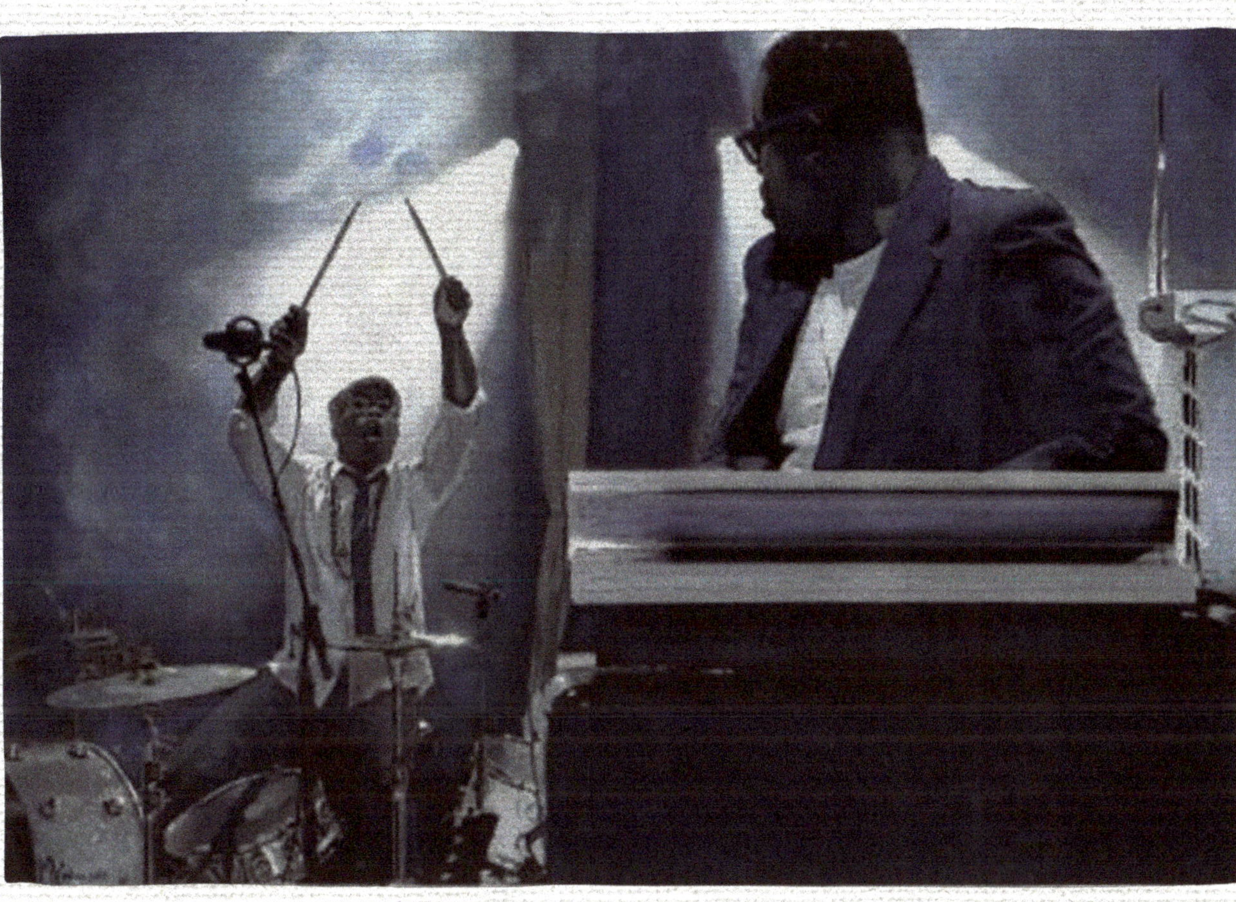

WHITE "TRASH TONGUE TALKER"

The name of this track is called "TRASH TONGUE TALKER" It's also from the Blunderbuss album (Jack White's first solo record.) We were just playing this groove and just jamming out. then I started messing around and came up with that little snare intro, that pattering, and Jack got excited and said we should use that for the beginning and the rest was history. This track we recorded in 2011. It was my first time coming to Jack's home studio and I was blown away. Memorable day for sure.

LIDELL "WALK RIGHT BACK"

The name of this track is called "WALK RIGHT BACK" and it was from Jamie Lidell's latest album called "Building a Beginning" which came out 2016. We recorded this at Sound Emporium in Nashville, TN. I remember he just had a chord playing on the keyboard and this was the beat that I just started playing on top. He pretty much just based the track around my drums. He added Pino Palladino on bass. I'm a big fan. He's worked with D'Angelo and The Who. This track was the first single from the album.

Jack White is also a drummer, but invited Daru to come in and bring his own flavor to the songs. Creativity is encouraged.

BAILEY "BREAKING"

The name of this track is called "BREAKING". It's by an artist from the UK named Liam Bailey from the album "Definitely Now" which came out in 2014. We recorded this track at Sears sound in New York, and I brought in my friend Brian Cochrane to play bass. Also brought in another friend, Sharif, to play guitar. We wrote this together and it's produced by a good friend of mine, Salaam Remi. It came out on Salaam's first independent record label Flying Buddha. This was a fun record. Had a good time making this record with everybody. My patterns are inspired by the track "Love and Happiness" by Al Green.

LORENZO "LA BOHÈME"

The name of this track is called "LA BOHÈME" by Italian artist Lorenzo Jovanotti from the album "2015 CC". We recorded this track at Jimi Hendrix studio Electric Lady in New York. Fun session. My drum pattern was inspired by Stevie Wonder's "Superstition" as you can hear.

> Daru says that it is a blessing to work with friends because it allows for a familiar and comfortable energy.

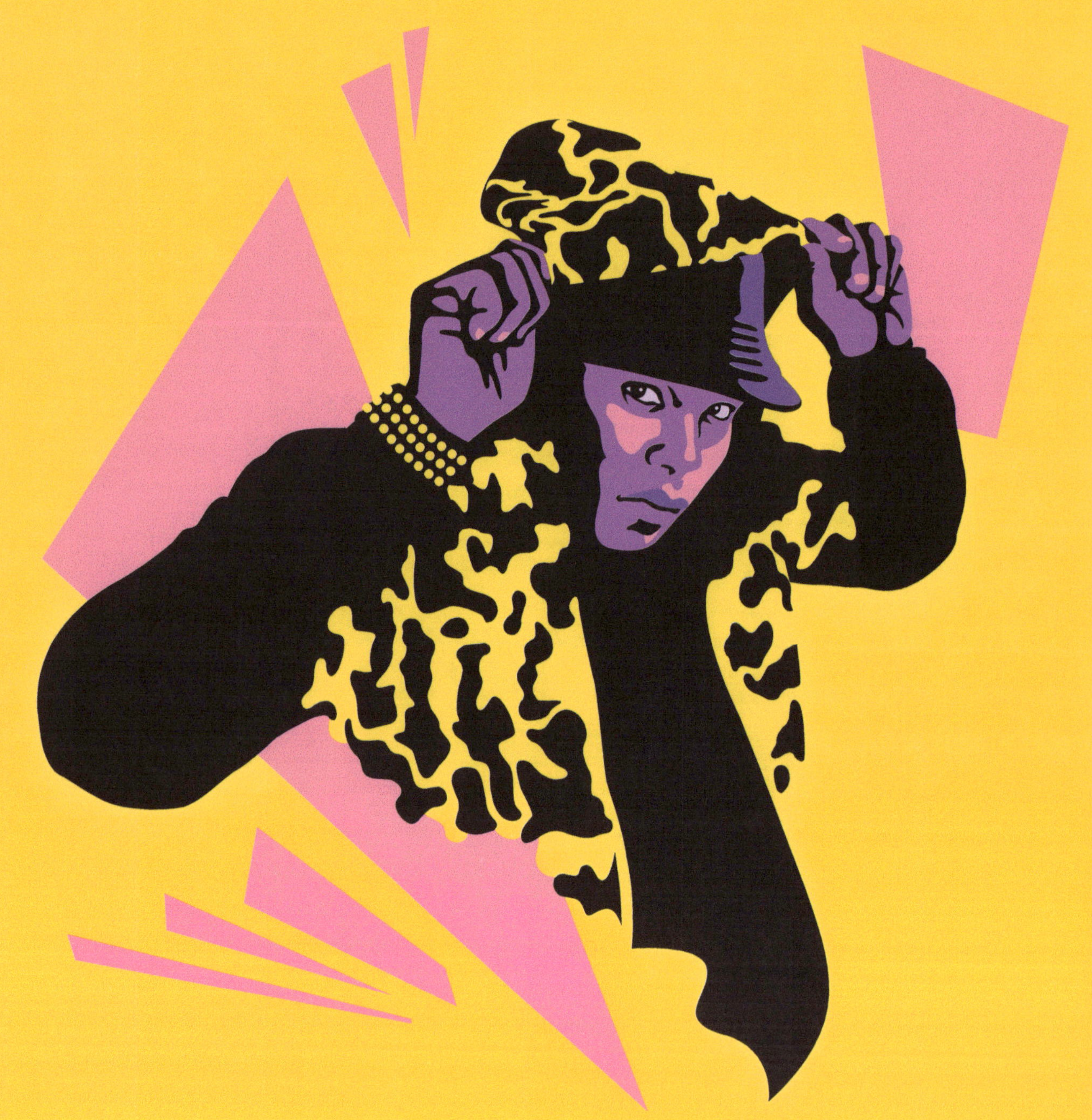

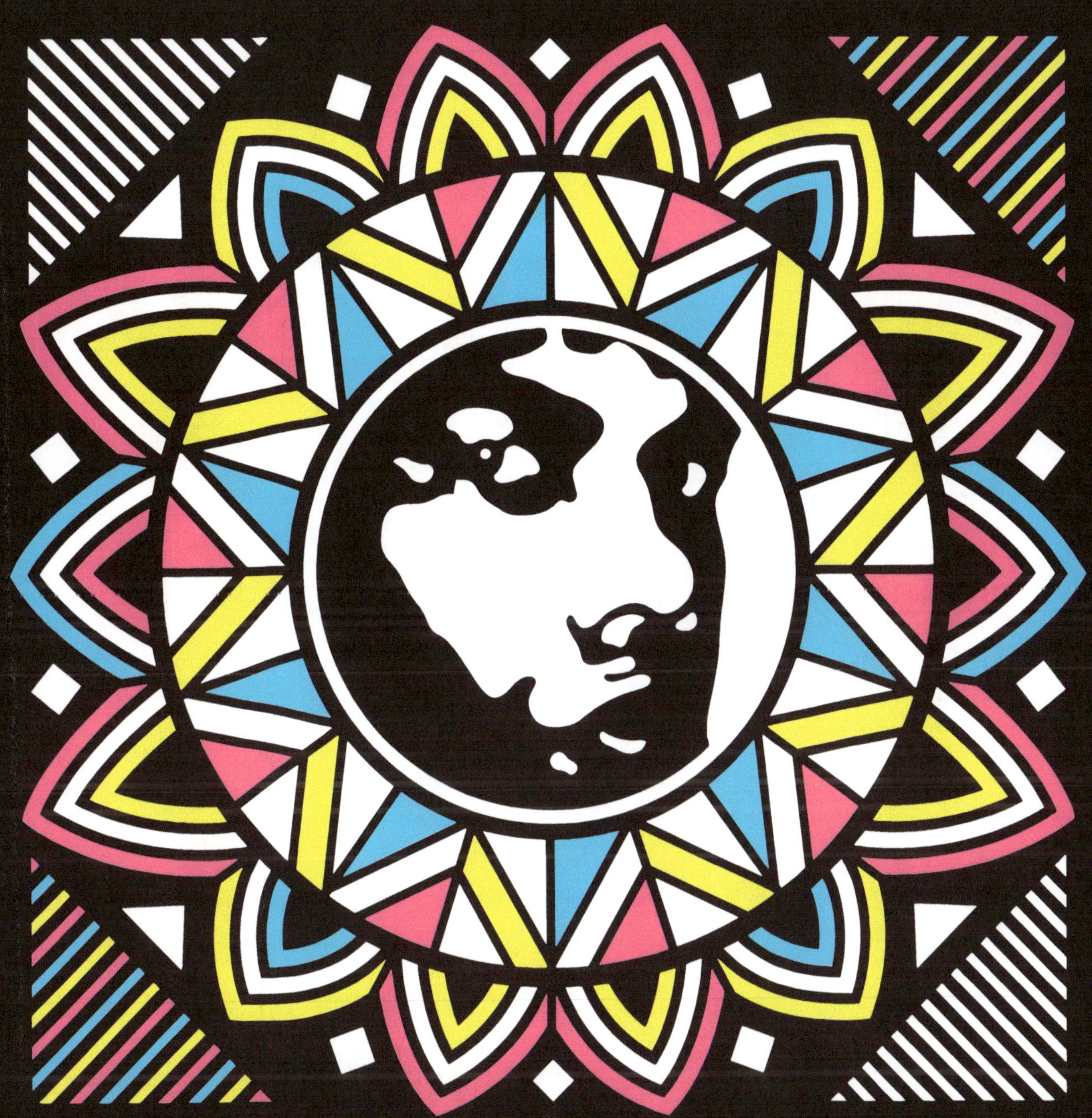

LORENZO "RAGAZZA MAGICA"

The name of this track is called "RAGAZZA MAGICA" (and I hope I'm pronouncing these Italian titles correctly.) This was another track from Lorenzo Jovanotti's "2015 CC", recorded at Electric Lady Studios in New York. We were listening to a bunch of 90s Soul and Hip-Hop music, and my drum pattern was inspired by the songs that we heard.

INVENTORS "CLOSER"

The name of this track is called "CLOSER" (featuring yours truly) by Modern Inventors. Each member of this group is from Philadelphia and New York. My friend Owen Biddle plays bass and he introduced me to the other members. Owen played with the Roots as well. My drum pattern was inspired by Jimi Hendrix "Little Miss Lover" and I just made up my own swag and approach.

Daru's style is inspired by an eclectic collection of musicians who came before him and inspired him.

NEON
"I'M GONNA GO AWAY NOW"

The name of this track is called "I'M GONNA GO AWAY NOW" (featuring myself and Phil Lassiter) by my good friend MonoNeon on his 2018 album "I Don't Care Today (Angels & Demons in Lo-Fi)." The drums came from these Converse Sample Packs that I did with Brandon Owens. I just sent Mono a bunch of breaks that I did and he added his own funk on top, and this is what we came up with for this collaboration.

NEON
"WHEN THE NEON PEARLY GATES OPEN"

The name of this track is called "WHEN THE NEON PEARLY GATES OPEN" and it's another track from my good friend MonoNeon's album "I Don't Care Today." The drums from this came from working with producer Young RJ from Detroit – we were working on some sketches for a new Slum Village record – I took the drums from the track that we laid because we wasn't gonna use it, and I sent them to Mono, and Mono laid a MEAN groove with this one. Definitely one of my favorites from the album. Yeah, it's a heater.

Daru has performed at some very unique locations, including pop-up shows at a gas station and laundromat with Jack White.

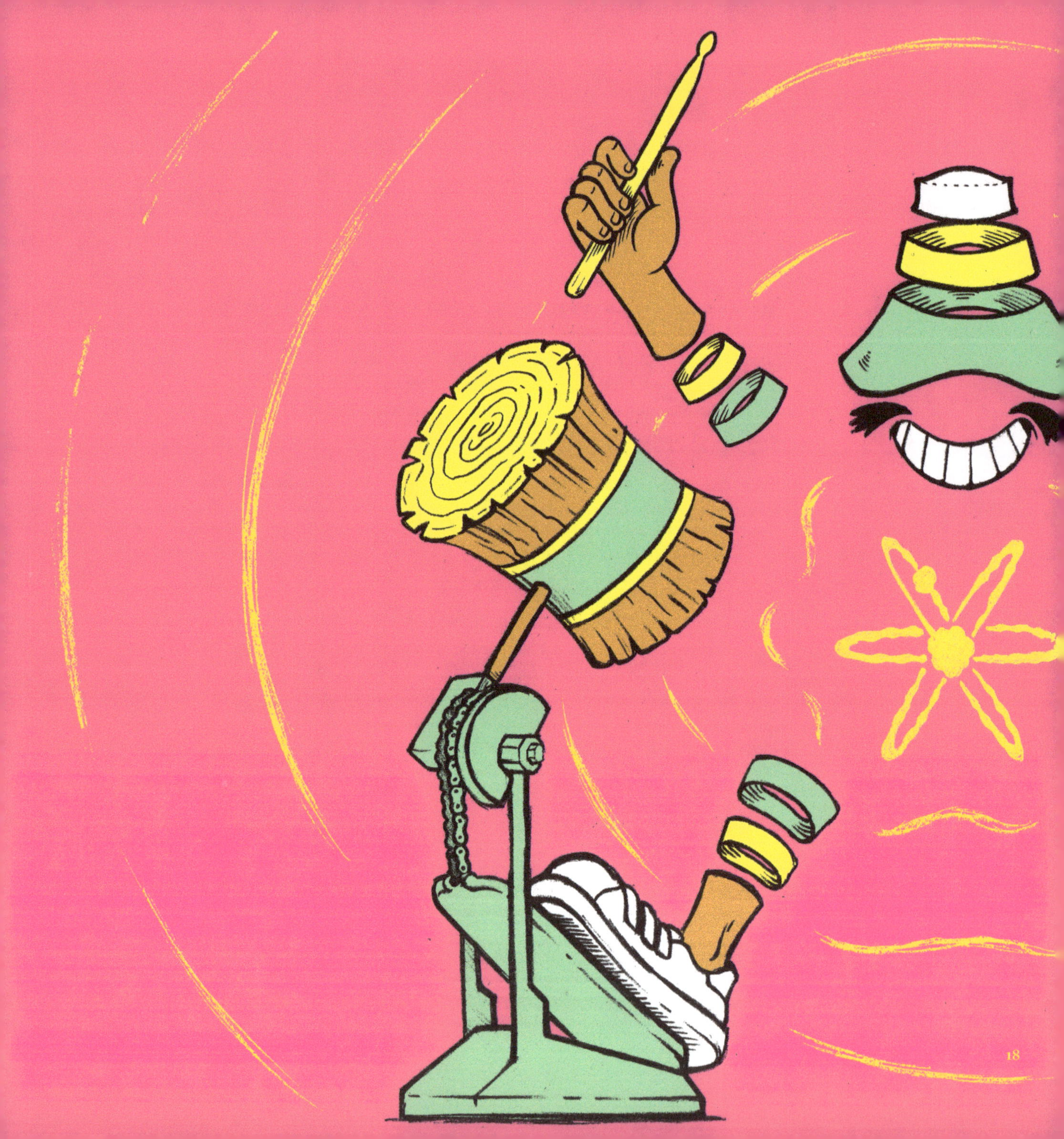

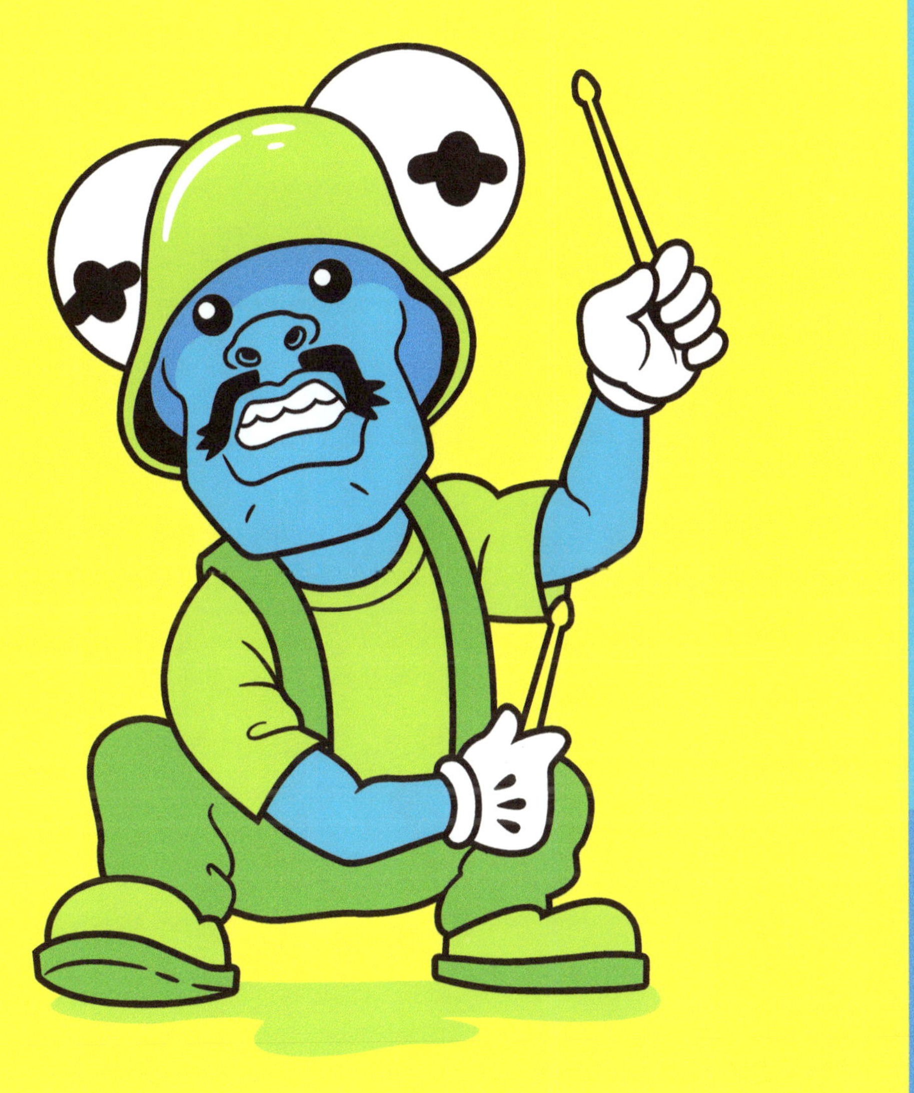

Nameless
"Let Me Live"

The name of this track is called "LET ME LIVE" and it's unreleased. A good friend of mine, Nameless feat. Nametag. Actually, I was supposed to finish this track forever ago. I think Nameless sent this to me like 2 years ago. It was a Barter, because Nameless does artwork and he's an amazing Illustrator, and this was a trade-off. Basically he would do my art covers and I would just trade him with drums. Finally got it done and this is what it is. The drum pattern was inspired by James Brown drummers (Clyde Stubblefield and "Jabo") just kind of played in my own swag and this is what I came up with for the record.

Rock
"Black Superhero Car"

The name of this track is called "BLACK SUPERHERO CAR" feat. Rick Ross. This is from the "Don't Smoke Rock" collaboration with Pete Rock and Smoke DZA. This was the project where a good friend of mine Pete Rock was having some problems clearing samples, and he asked me if I would put together some musicians so we could replay the samples. I just replayed the drum pattern that he produced, and this is one of my favorite cuts from the album.

Daru believes that creativity is what keeps us evolving.

ROCK "I AIN'T SCARED"

This is another track from the "Don't Smoke Rock" album with Pete Rock and Smoke DZA. It came out in 2016. The name of the song is called "I AIN'T SCARED". It's one of my favorites. Actually, Pete Rock raps on this track and again I just replayed the drum patterns that he originally made and this is what it is.

VILLAGE "WHERE WE COME FROM"

The name of this track is called "WHERE WE COME FROM." It's by Slum Village and the album is called "YES!" It came out in 2015. I had been building with one of my favorite producers from Detroit Young RJ and we finally got a chance to work together. He sent me this track and the original drums came from Aretha Franklin's "Rocksteady" Rest in Peace. This was a famous drum break and I just replayed it with my own swag, and they basically just brought in my part of a groove at the end of the record where it becomes instrumental. Really cool part of the song.

From a young age, Daru was able to hear a song one time and be able to play it... until he was introduced to more complex jazz songs.

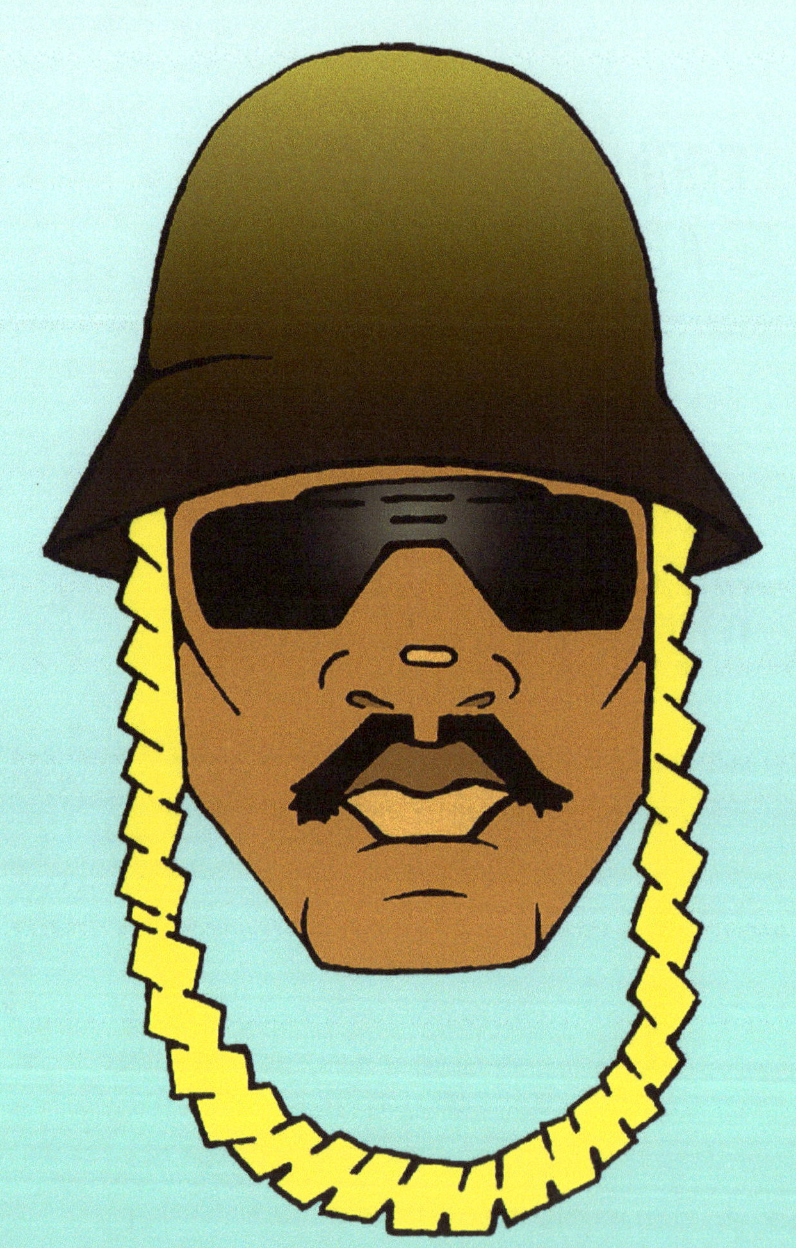

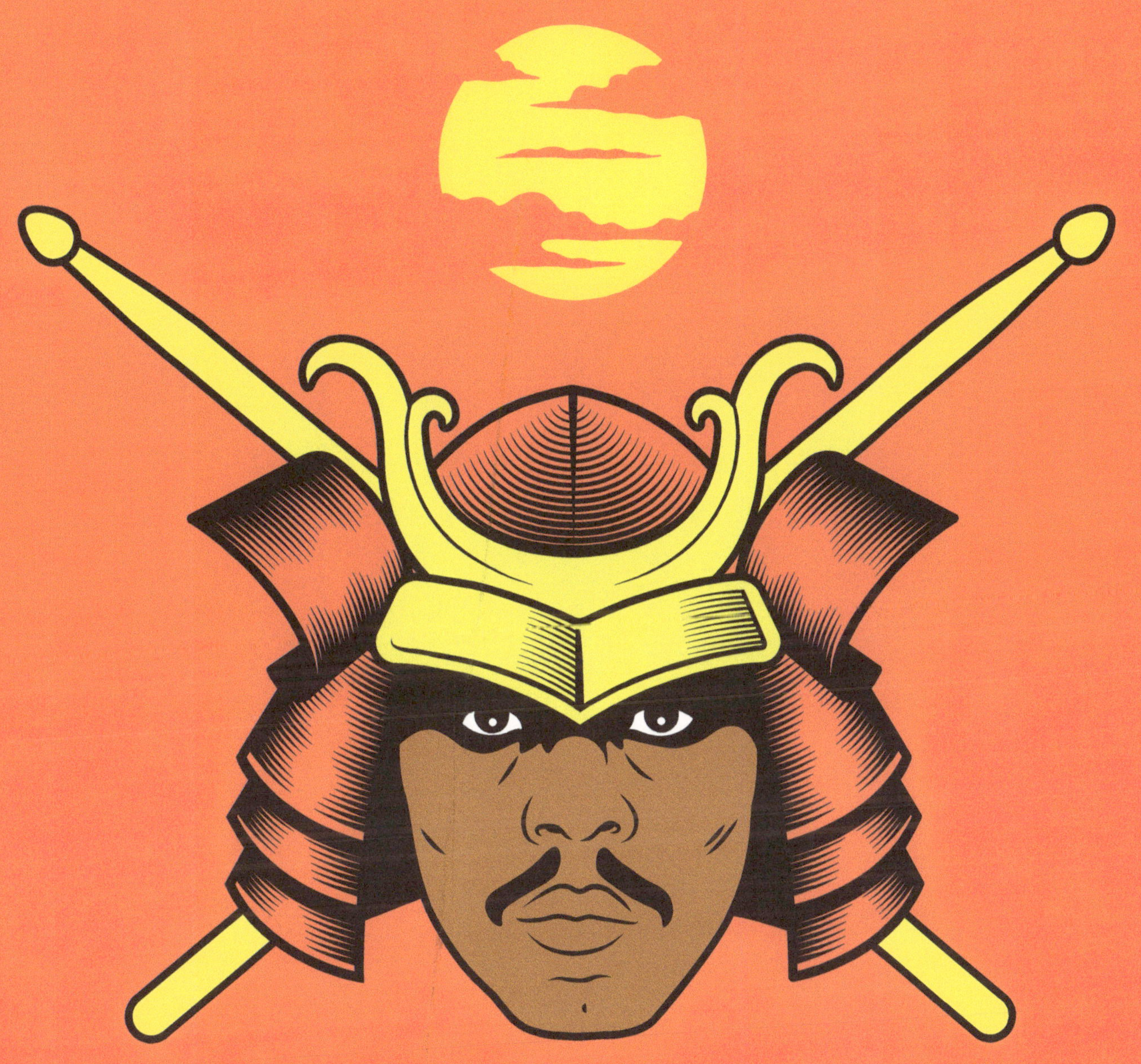

KWELI
"COLD RAIN"

The name of this track is called "COLD RAIN" by Talib Kwali from the album "Gutter Rainbows" (2011). Produced by the homie, Ski Beatz. I was a member of Ski's band called The Senseis and we recorded this at Dame Dash Art Gallery Studios – The Dojo right in the basement. This was a fun session. Rest in Peace John Cave. Ski had the track and I just replayed the pattern that he had already produced on the drums. That's how this one came about.

PACK
"FUNKY FRESH"

The name of this track is called "FUNKY FRESH" and it's from the Beats EP 2015. I did this track with the group The Ruff Pack. My drum pattern was inspired by Parliament, George Clinton, a lot of those records. That was the vibe. This is what I came up with.

> You never knew who was going to come through the Dojo. Many celebrities would hang out at this hidden SoHo gem, also called "only 100" due to its 100 person limited capacity.

PACK "L.T.A.I."

The name of this track is called "L.T.A.I." and it means "Let's Talk About It". This was a track that I produced for the group The Ruff Pack. The beat came from an old cassette tape of some production that I'd done in the early 2000s and I just brought the track to them. Then we just pretty much replayed what I sampled and the same drum pattern. We added a different section to it. Really cool track from that album.

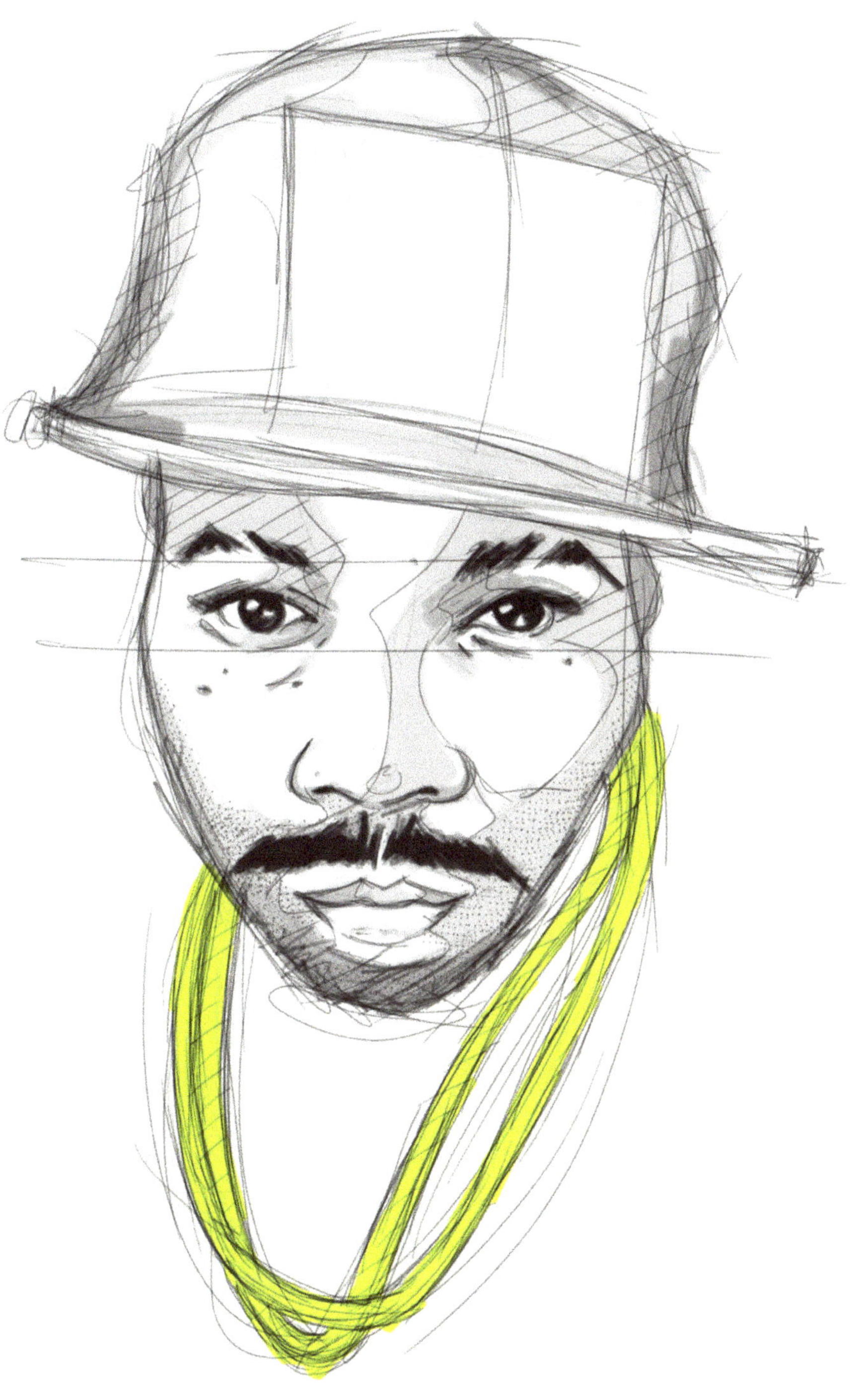

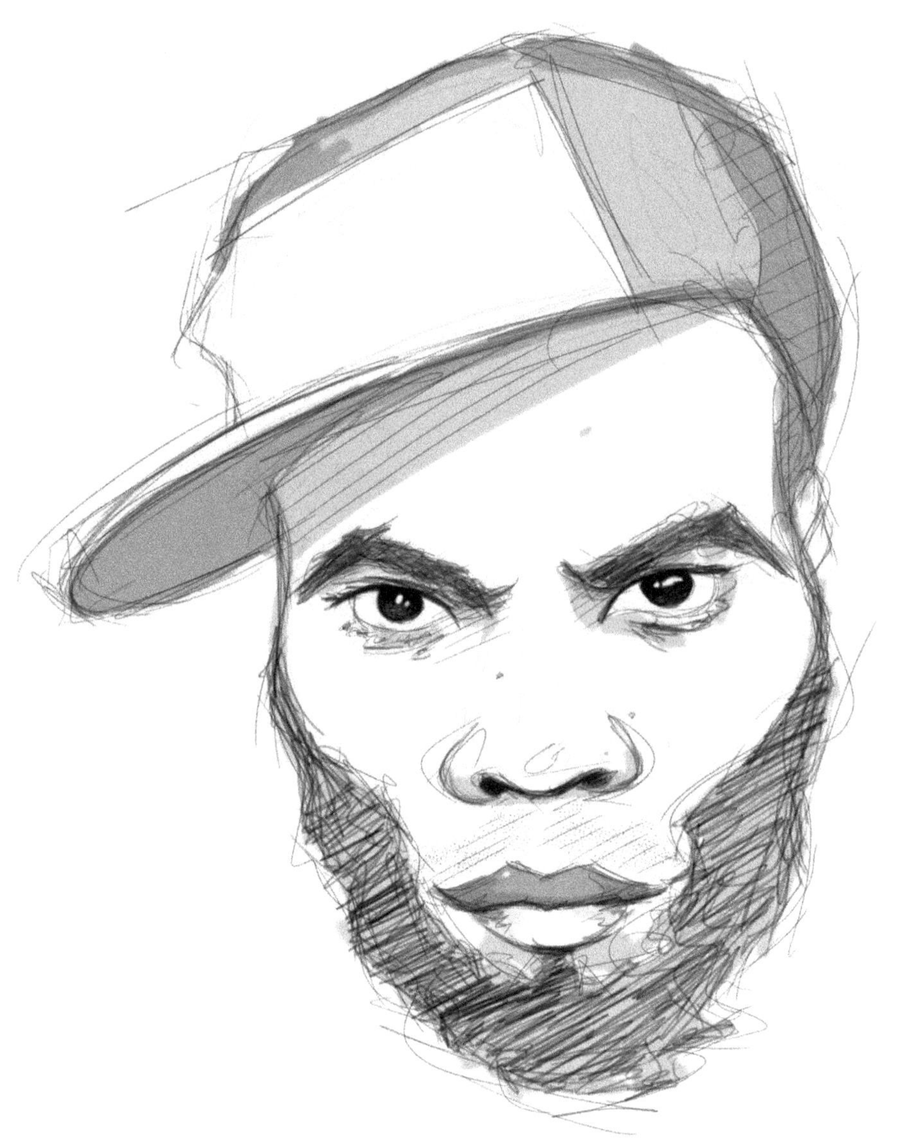

RJ "HUH?!"

The name of this track is called "HUH?!" It's by Young RJ from his debut release "Blaq Royalty" and it came out in 2017. This was a fun one. This is one of those skeletons we originally created for Slum Village, but he ended up using it for the solo record. This is the signature Daru Jones vibe on the rhythms. It worked out. The track was based around my drums and he added samples on top.

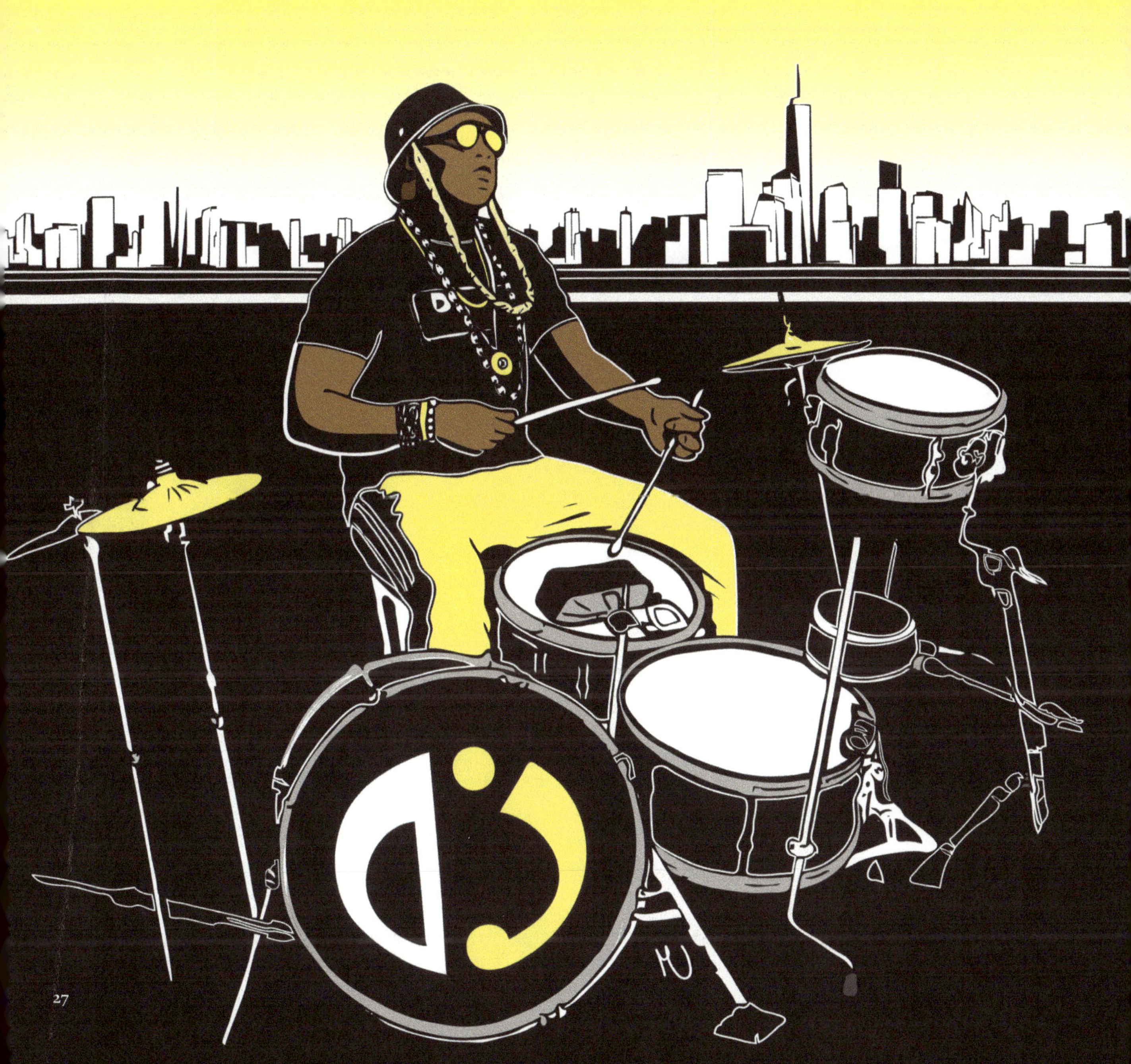

C$Y "MONTREUX"

The name of this track is called "MONTREUX" by Curren$y from "Pilot Talk II." It came out in 2010 and is produced by Ski Beatz.

PACK "WITH YOU"

The name of this song is called "WITH YOU" and it's from the self-titled release. Another song from the Ruff Pack that came out in 2013. We actually recorded this track in Austria and the guys already had the tune together. I was trying to think of a pattern that would work for the whole track and this is what worked. It's one of my favorite songs off the album. It's the second track and this is what it is.

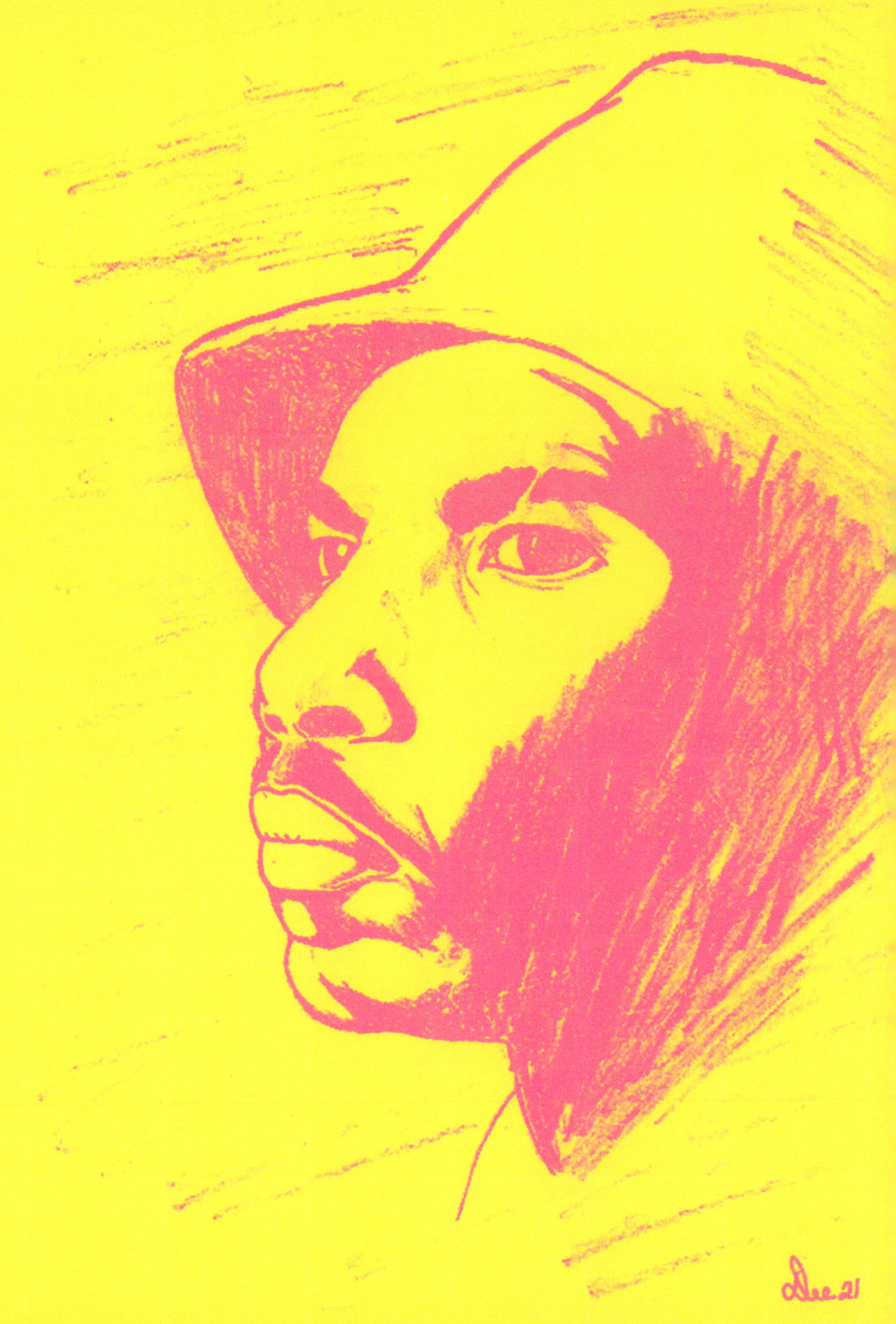

JONES "EPILOGUE"

My name is Daru Jones. I had the pleasure of recording these Breaks at the Layman Drug Company in Nashville, TN. Big shout out to the head of operations Will Greig and chief engineer Tony Moglia. Thanks for checking out "Daru Jones *Play the Breaks*: Live from Layman." Hoping you guys enjoy what I've done and I definitely am thankful for all the artists that allow me to use my creative artistry on these records.

Cheers!

Daru Jones

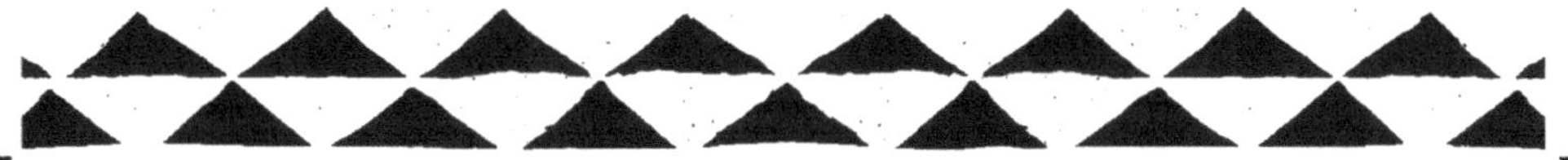

Recorded at Layman Drug Company (Nashville, TN) 2018

Mixed by **Ben Kane** @ Electric Garden Recording Studios (*Brooklyn, NY*)

EQ'ed & Mastered by **BreakBeat Lou**

Head of Operations: **Will Greg**

Tracking Assistant Engineer: **Tony Moglia**

Book Design: **Tristan McNatt**

Cover Photos: **Nick L. Photo**

Deluxe Edition Publisher & Interviewer: **Morissa Schwartz**

Signature Drums & Gear:

"DJNY" Daru Jones New Yorker Pacific Drums

"PST X DJ's 45" Paiste Cymbals

DJNY "Leo Sticks" Ahead Drumsticks

"Neo Blaq" Daru Jones LoFReQ Solomon Mics

Latin Percussion

Remo Drumheads

Illustrations:

Dee Jones – Pages 1,29

Saul "Lemon Drops N Cherry Bombs" McCoy – Pages 3, 19

Mary Vernaz – Pages 7, 11, 27

Tristan McNatt – Pages 10, 14, 15, 18, 23

Nameless – Pages 22, 25, 26

Beth J – Page 6

www.ingramcontent.com/pod-product-compliance
Lightning Source LLC
LaVergne TN
LVHW060628110826
845147LV00015B/964

* 9 7 8 1 9 5 8 5 0 3 1 0 2 *